EXPLOSIVES TECHNICIANS

Trudy Becker

Apex is distributed by North Star Editions:
sales@northstareditions.com | 888-417-0195

Produced for Apex by Red Line Editorial.

Photographs ©: Shutterstock Images, cover, 1, 4–5, 8–9, 10–11, 12–13, 14–15, 18–19, 20–21, 24–25, 30–31, 32–33, 34–35, 38–39, 42–43, 44–45, 46–47, 48–49, 50–51, 54–55, 56–57, 58; Library of Congress, 6–7; Sascha Schuermann/Getty Images News/Getty Images, 16–17; China Photos/Getty Images News/Getty Images, 22–23; Mario Tama/Getty Images News/Getty Images, 26–27; Elaine Thompson/AP Images, 29; iStockphoto, 37, 52–53; Charles Trusler/Topical Press Agency/Hulton Archive/Getty Images, 41

Library of Congress Control Number: 2025930338

ISBN
979-8-89250-669-4 (hardcover)
979-8-89250-703-5 (ebook pdf)
979-8-89250-687-8 (hosted ebook)

Printed in the United States of America
Mankato, MN
082025

NOTE TO PARENTS AND EDUCATORS

Apex books are designed to build literacy skills in striving readers. Exciting, high-interest content attracts and holds readers' attention. The text is carefully leveled to allow students to achieve success quickly.

TABLE OF CONTENTS

Kennesaw Mountain National Battlefield Park has more than 20 miles (32 km) of trails.

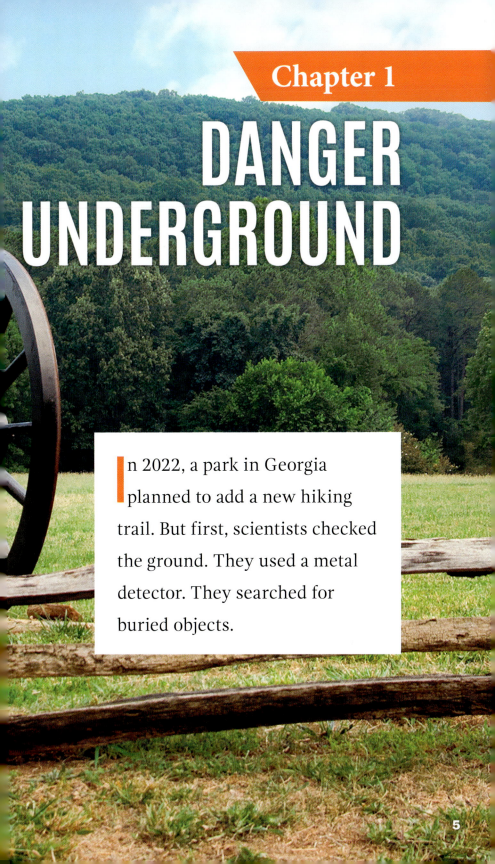

Chapter 1

DANGER UNDERGROUND

In 2022, a park in Georgia planned to add a new hiking trail. But first, scientists checked the ground. They used a metal detector. They searched for buried objects.

The scientists found an old, rusty explosive. They uncovered it carefully. Then a bomb squad came to help. They removed the explosive from the ground. Then they took it away. They disposed of it safely.

CANNON FIRE

The explosive was a shell from a type of cannon called a Parrott gun. It came from the US Civil War (1861–1865). Workers found it in Kennesaw Mountain National Battlefield Park. Soldiers fought there in 1864. The shell came from this battle.

The Union Army used Parrott guns to fire many shells during the US Civil War (1861–1865).

Chapter 2

MANY TYPES

Explosives technicians work with things that can blow up. Some explosives are weapons. Examples include bombs, grenades, and shells. These weapons can cause massive damage. They shoot out sharp pieces. Some can knock down buildings or start fires.

A grenade is a type of small bomb. To set it off, people pull a pin.

Some technicians work to stop this damage. The techs try to find explosives before they blow up. Techs may take the explosives apart. Or they may plan ways to blow things up without hurting people.

EARLY EXPLOSIVES

Chinese people invented gunpowder in the 800s. By the 900s, people were using it to make exploding weapons. At first, people mainly used cannons. Guns and grenades became common in the 1500s. By the mid-1900s, many armies dropped large bombs.

A technician works to remove a bomb that was placed near a car.

However, not all explosives are weapons. Fireworks are one example. They create beautiful showers of sparks. But they can also be dangerous. So, experts light them off. These workers are a type of technician.

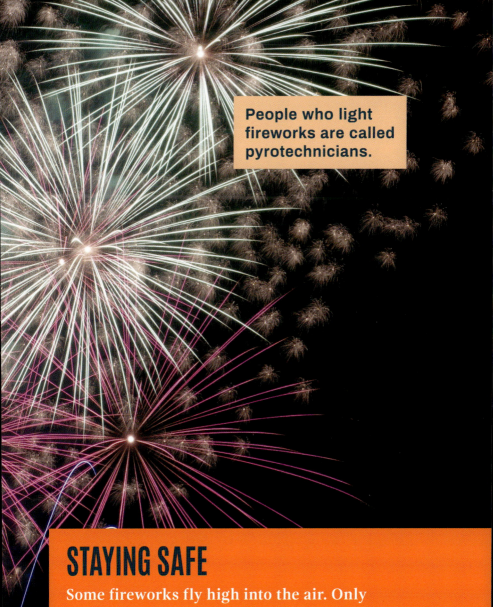

People who light fireworks are called pyrotechnicians.

STAYING SAFE

Some fireworks fly high into the air. Only experts should light this type. If something goes wrong, the fireworks can blow up early. Or burning pieces can hit the ground. People can get badly hurt. Experts train to prevent this. They also work in teams. They help one another watch for problems.

In fact, several jobs involve setting off explosions on purpose. Some explosions help control avalanches. Many mountains have deep snow. When thick snow piles up, it can become unstable. It may break apart and crash down. The falling snow moves quickly. It can bury people and buildings. To prevent this, workers use explosives to set off a small avalanche. That way, they can plan where the snow slides. And a bigger avalanche is less likely to happen.

Workers create small explosions to prevent big avalanches.

Other workers help with construction. Some plan explosions to demolish buildings, bridges, or other structures. Others clear land for roads and trails. They may blast through rocks or fallen trees to clear the way.

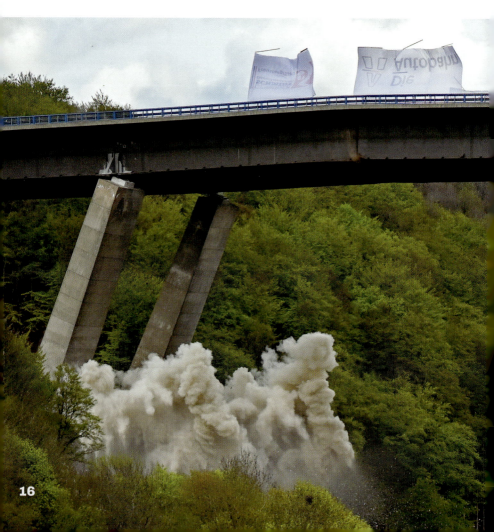

SKY HIGH

In 2017, workers started to tear down the CPF Building. This skyscraper was in Singapore. It stood 561 feet (171 m) tall. It had more than 40 floors. It was one of the 10 tallest buildings ever demolished.

Workers used explosives to demolish the Rahmede Valley Bridge in Germany in 2023.

Chapter 3

BLASTING

Workers who set off explosions are sometimes called blasters. They are often hired to demolish old buildings. These buildings may be weak or damaged. Or people may want to use the space for something else.

Blasters often help tear down old apartment buildings.

Blasters plan how to knock each building down. They study the building's support structures. Those parts hold the building up. Blasters plan ways to remove them. They use explosives such as dynamite.

BIT BY BIT

Blasters often divide a building into sections. They place explosives near each section's bottom. When these explosives go off, higher parts of the building collapse. They fall down or cave inward.

If a few levels of a building are blasted, higher parts will fall down on top of them.

Blasters may destroy other structures, too. For instance, dams sometimes need to be removed or replaced. Big dams are demolished in stages. Workers remove small sections one by one. That lets the water flow out slowly. The process can take months or years.

FAILED FALL

Sometimes, blasters get it wrong. That happened in 2009 in Liuzhou, China. Blasters split a building in half. One half leaned dangerously. The other half crashed to the ground. It fell sideways.

葛洲坝集 cgac   C围堰爆破圆满成功

While building the Three Gorges Dam in China, workers built a cofferdam to help hold back water. They blew up this cofferdam in 2006.

Some blasters use explosions to change the shape of land. They often help with construction projects. For example, houses need foundations. Blasters may flatten an area of land. Then other workers build houses there.

Blasters drill patterns of holes that hold explosives. They plan how to break the rock into chunks.

People also use explosives to create tunnels. Workers drill holes into hills, cliffs, or mountains. Blasters put explosives in the holes. The explosions crack the rock. People clear away the broken pieces. Then they can build roads or railways.

Blasting is a key part of mining, too. Mining companies may drill deep holes in the ground. They put explosives at the bottom. The blasts create caves. Other times, companies do mountaintop removal (MTR) mining. They blast away a big chunk of a mountain.

Many coal mines in the Appalachian Mountains use mountaintop removal.

MANGLED MOUNTAIN

MTR blasts away hundreds of feet of a mountain. It creates tons of rubble. Often, this gets dumped nearby. MTR also sends out harmful chemicals. Nearby people, plants, and animals can get sick or die.

DAM DANGER

Glines Canyon Dam was built in the early 1900s. It helped hold back the Elwha River in Washington. But over time, the dam caused problems. It blocked fish and flooded some areas. So, in 2011, people started to remove it.

At first, workers chipped away parts of the dam. This let some water drain out. Then they used explosives. They blew up concrete near the bottom. They worked slowly. That way, rushing water wouldn't hurt people. Neither would falling pieces.

It took three years to fully remove the Glines Canyon Dam.

Chapter 4

BOMB SQUADS

Workers who try to prevent explosions are sometimes called bomb techs. They may work in groups called bomb squads. But they handle many types of explosives. Examples include land mines and IEDs.

A pipe bomb is a type of IED that is made from a piece of pipe.

Tons of explosives from World War II are still left today.

Some bomb squads work for militaries. Enemies may fire grenades or drop bombs. They may also bury explosives underground. Bomb squads try to keep these things from blowing up. They may use metal detectors or lasers to search areas. They remove any explosives they find.

WARTIME LEFTOVERS

During World War II (1939–1945), armies dropped bombs around the world. They buried many land mines, too. Some are still in or on the ground. If they explode, they can hurt people very badly. Technicians work to find and remove them.

Some bomb squads are part of police forces. Others work for governments. These squads often respond to threats. For example, a person may place a bomb near a building. A squad will rush to the scene to help.

First, techs move people out of the area. Then they examine the bomb. They try to learn how it works.

BOMB DOGS

Dogs help some bomb techs find explosives. The dogs are trained to recognize how explosives smell. Techs bring the dogs to an area. The dogs sniff around. They bark or signal if they find something.

Bomb squads may be called if someone finds a bag or box that might be a bomb.

Next, techs use tools to stop the bomb from causing damage. For some bombs, techs use disruptors. These machines shoot at bombs. Some fire metal ammo. Others spray water. Disruptors can damage a bomb's wires. Or they can make the bomb blow up safely when no people are around.

Techs place disruptors near bombs. Then they step back. They can fire the disruptors from a safe distance.

Some bombs have more than one way to explode. So, techs try not to stay near bombs for very long. Techs may go near to take X-rays or place tools. But they move away soon after.

Disruptors often look like long, metal tubes.

In some cases, techs must work up close. Deminers are one example. These techs disarm mines. They often snip wires to cut the power supply. They wear heavy suits and face shields for protection.

BOMB ROBOTS

Bomb techs often use robots. The robots are remote-controlled. Bomb techs steer robots toward bombs. Then they use the robots' arms and tools to defuse bombs. Robots also carry cameras so techs can see what they're doing.

Bomb robots often have claws that can grip and carry things.

DIGGING OUT

In 1940, World War II was raging. A bomb fell near St. Paul's Cathedral in London, England. The bomb sank deep into the ground. It didn't explode. But it could have gone off at any time.

Soldiers carefully dug it out. They worked not to hit anything that could trigger an explosion. After three days, they got the bomb out. A man took it far from the city. He set it off there. That way, no one got hurt when it exploded.

German planes dropped many bombs on London during World War II.

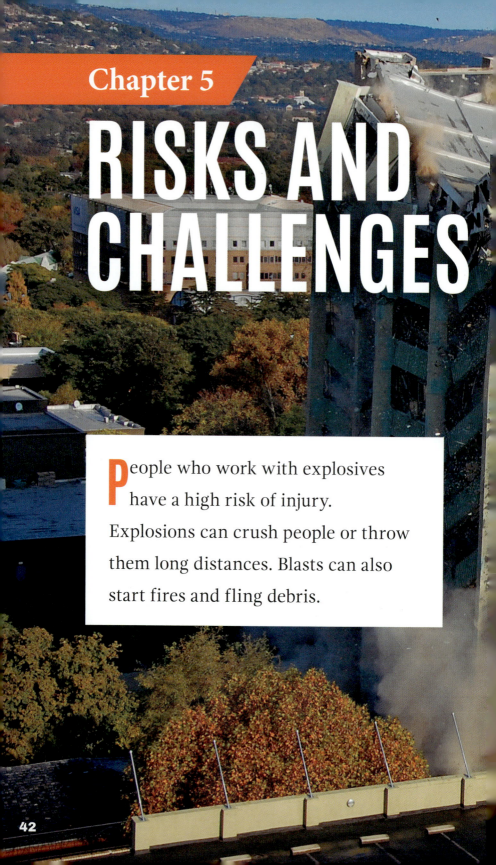

Chapter 5

RISKS AND CHALLENGES

People who work with explosives have a high risk of injury. Explosions can crush people or throw them long distances. Blasts can also start fires and fling debris.

When a building collapses, falling debris can hurt or kill people if it hits them.

Blasters try to guess which way a building might tip or fall.

Even a small mistake can cause big problems. So, technicians must be very careful. They plan how much power to use. If blasters use too much power, an explosion can get out of control. But using too little can also create danger. A building may stay standing but be unstable. It may collapse in ways people can't control.

LOSING POWER

In 2010, blasters placed explosives at the base of a tower in Ohio. The tower had a crack that blasters didn't see. When the explosives went off, this crack made the tower unsteady. It toppled down in the wrong direction. It crashed through power lines. Thousands of people lost power.

For bomb techs, time is a huge challenge. Many bombs are hooked up to timers. The timers may have already started when bomb techs arrive. Or techs may accidentally start timers as they work. Sometimes, techs have less than a minute to finish the job.

BOMB TYPES

Some bombs explode when touched. Others are set to go off after a certain amount of time. People may also control bombs. They press a switch or button to blow them up.

Bomb techs train to do their jobs quickly before timers run out.

People wear thick suits while defusing bombs. Their hands are left free so they can be as precise as possible.

But speed is also risky. When people rush, they are more likely to make mistakes. Techs might bump or jostle a bomb. Or they might make a wrong guess about how it works. Both can make the bomb go off.

Safety gear helps protect people from some heat and damage. But workers can still be badly hurt or killed.

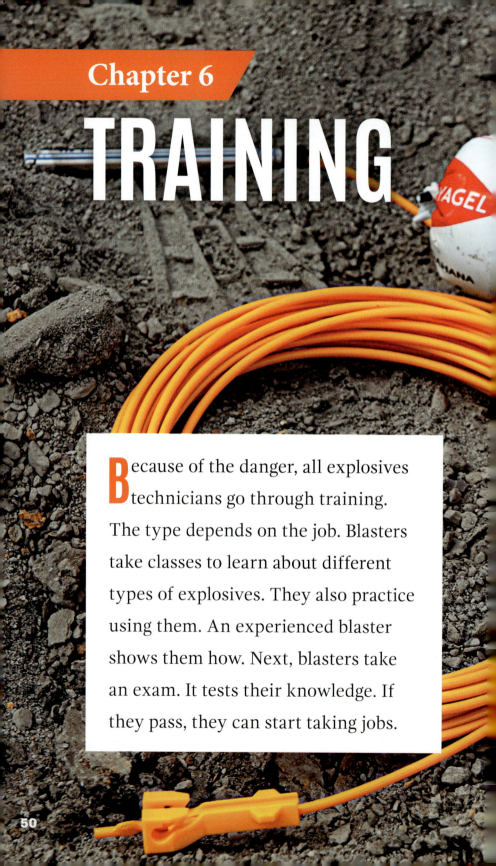

Chapter 6
TRAINING

Because of the danger, all explosives technicians go through training. The type depends on the job. Blasters take classes to learn about different types of explosives. They also practice using them. An experienced blaster shows them how. Next, blasters take an exam. It tests their knowledge. If they pass, they can start taking jobs.

Blasters often connect wires to explosives to help control when they go off.

Bomb techs often are part of police forces or militaries. So, these groups handle their training. The first step is basic training. All police officers and soldiers go through this. It teaches the basic rules of the group. And it helps people build the skills they need, such as running quickly or firing weapons. After basic training, people begin learning more specific skills.

In the military, basic training is sometimes called boot camp.

During training, people practice searching an area for explosives.

Bomb-tech training includes several parts. Trainees take classes about bomb science. They learn how to identify and handle bombs. Then they put their skills into practice. For some tasks, they use fake bombs. But they may also work with real explosives.

FBI TECHS

The FBI runs a training program. It is called the Hazardous Devices School. It lasts six weeks. People who complete it often work with local police. They are called to help when people find something that might be a bomb.

At the end, trainees get a certification. This shows that they are ready to work.

However, explosives technology is always changing. People keep creating new types of bombs. They also find new ways to defuse them. So, most bomb techs redo their certification every couple of years. That helps them stay prepared for the latest threats.

RAVEN'S CHALLENGE

Raven's Challenge is a training event that takes place each year. It teaches bomb techs about new technology and tools. And it helps them practice responding to threats.

A robot removes a bomb from a car during a training event.

✓ SKILLS CHECKLIST

- Being willing to face danger to help others

- Having steady hands

- Knowing and following safety guidelines

- Staying calm under pressure

- Thinking quickly but carefully

- Understanding the science behind how explosives work

COMPREHENSION QUESTIONS

Write your answers on a separate piece of paper.

1. Write a few sentences explaining the main idea of Chapter 4.

2. Would you want to work as an explosives technician? Why or why not?

3. What does a disruptor do?
   A. shoots at a bomb
   B. helps people find bombs
   C. blows up part of a building

4. How could using robots help bomb techs stay safer?
   A. The techs could get closer to the bombs.
   B. The techs could stay farther from the bombs.
   C. The robots could carry the techs to the bombs.

5. What does **unstable** mean in this book?

When thick snow piles up, it can become
unstable. It may break apart and crash down.

    A. likely to fall

    B. likely to stay together

    C. likely to cost a lot

6. What does **support** mean in this book?

Blasters plan how to knock each building down.
They study the building's support structures.
Those parts hold the building up.

    A. used to make something weak

    B. used to keep something strong

    C. used to break something apart

Answer key on page 64.

GLOSSARY

avalanches
Times when lots of snow falls quickly down the side of a mountain.

construction
Work that involves building something.

debris
Pieces of something that broke or fell apart.

defuse
To remove part of a bomb so that it won't explode.

demolish
To knock down a large structure.

disposed
Got rid of something.

explosive
A device that can blow up, such as a bomb.

foundations
Bases that provide support for buildings.

IEDs
Short for "improvised explosive devices," these are handmade bombs.

lasers
Devices that shine strong beams of light. If that light bounces back, it can show what objects are nearby.

rubble
Broken chunks, often of rock, made by an explosion.

signal
To use an action to tell people something.

TO LEARN MORE

BOOKS

Chandler, Matt. *Robotics*. Bellwether Media, 2022.

Hamilton, John. *K9*. Abdo Publishing, 2022.

Marlin, Charles. *Bombers*. Apex Editions, 2025.

ONLINE RESOURCES

Visit **www.apexeditions.com** to find links and resources related to this title.

ABOUT THE AUTHOR

Trudy Becker lives in Minneapolis, Minnesota. She loves fireworks but avoids most other explosives.

INDEX

ANSWER KEY:

1. Answers will vary; 2. Answers will vary; 3. A; 4. B; 5. A; 6. B